The Golden Star Alliance is an
aspect of the Council of the
Stellar Ring here to support
the emergence of
a new civilization
and species of beings
who live lives dedicated
to Spirit and the ascension
into immortal bodies of Light,
and to assist in
the ecstatic transformation
of Planet Earth into a Star.

This book, formerly titled "Light Body Facilitation...
In Support of a World in Transition," was originally channeled through Zarantra, another aspect of the extraterrestrial Spirit now known as ZāRah.

Golden Star Publishing
and
Golden Star Alliance
are outreach projects of U.L.C. Inc.

Our new address:
Golden Star Alliance
1410 Forest Dr. #8, Suite 133
Annapolis, MD 21403
(800) 576-1669

Printed by
MISSION POSSIBLE
COMMERCIAL PRINTING
P. O. Box 1495 · Sedona, AZ 86339
(520) 282-6523

I'M O.K.

I'm Just Mutating!

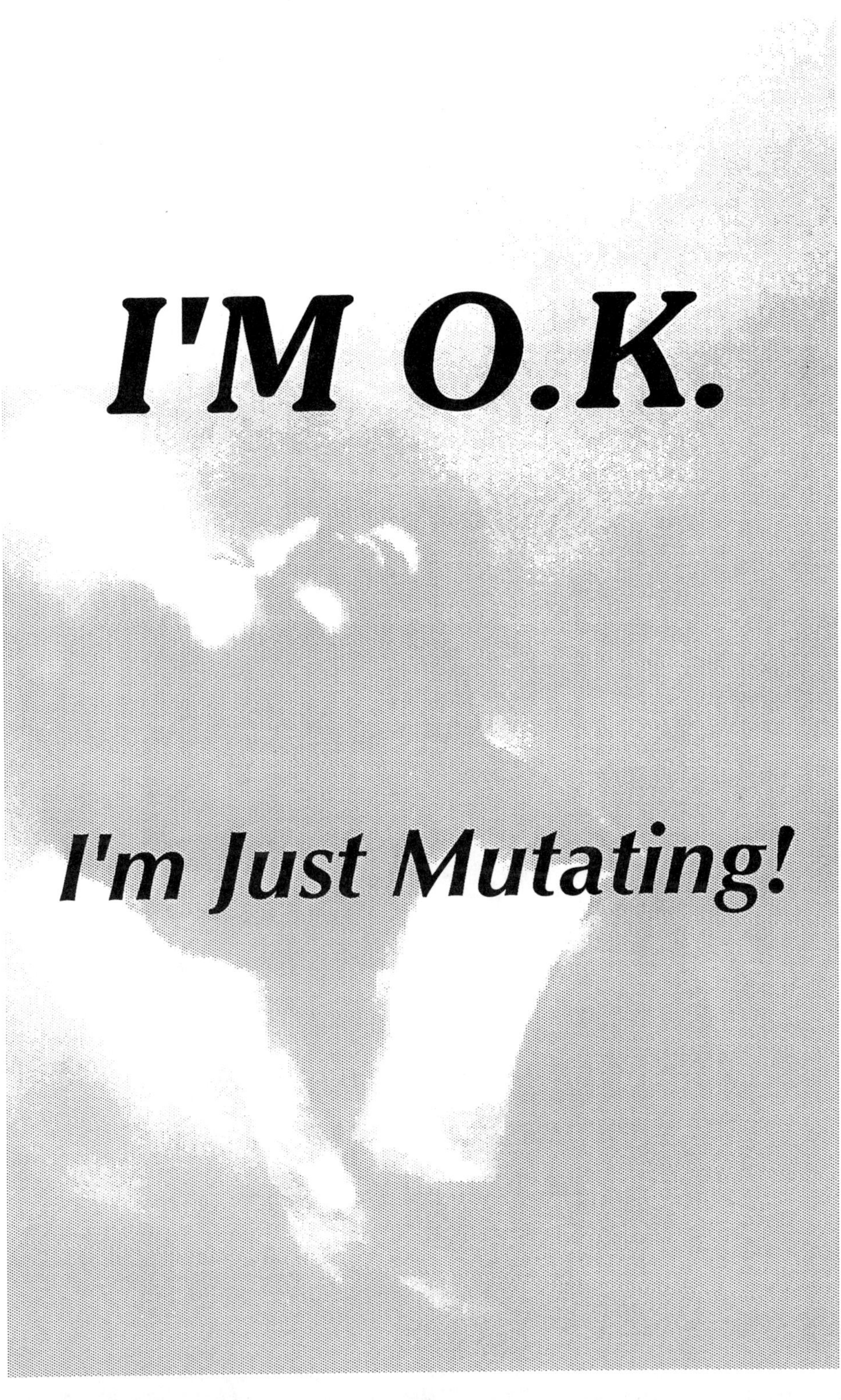

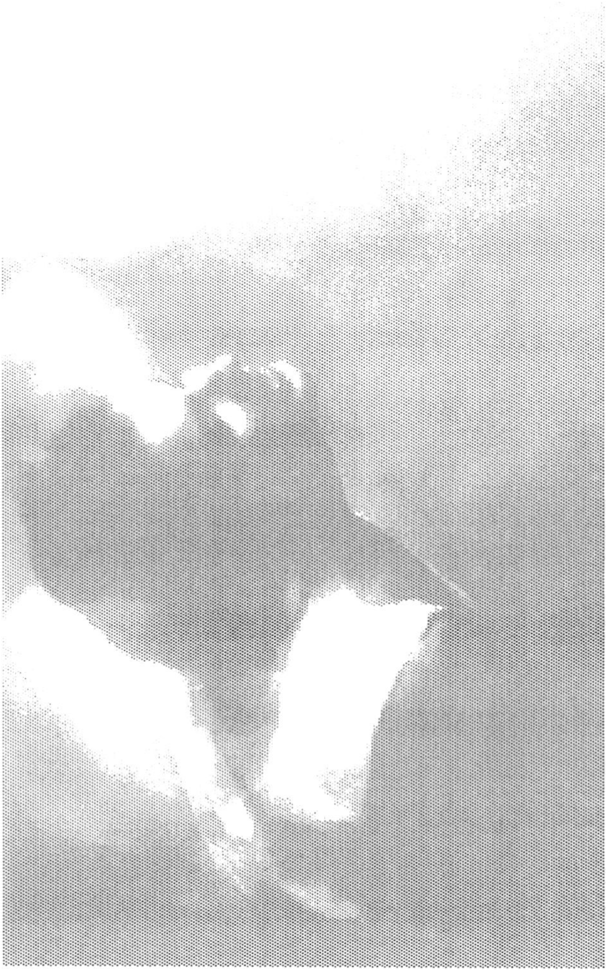

"It is time to wake up to
the vast multi-dimensional
master that you are."

Table of Contents

I'm O.K. I'm Just Mutating!

The Ecstatic Transformation

Major shifts are now taking place upon this planet. Never before have such accelerated energies been available to you. Many of you wake up each day disillusioned with jobs, careers and lifestyles. You have a feeling, an intuition, a *knowing* that there is more to life. You have been searching for that, yearning for it. Well, the good news is...*Never before has it been so easy to fulfill your Divine Mission and Purpose here.*

Much of the energy now coming to the Earth plane is new and unfamiliar to you. As more and more light becomes available, new pathways need to be cut to incorporate these higher frequencies. In the meantime they are having a profound effect on all beings here. The cells of your body have never before experienced such rapid states of transmutation. As a species you are evolving more in this one lifetime than ever before.

We have come here at this time to support beings in the ecstatic transformation that is taking place. Many of you also chose to come here to assist with this process. Now is the time to release the armor of dysfunctionality that you have been wearing, and to step forward into the Light of your Magnificence.

We would like to tell you a story. It may help you to remember....

—— The Cosmic Day ——

Once upon a time we were all part of one magnificent glowing orb of golden light. And ALL THAT IS, in Its desire for even more knowingness of ALL THAT IS, decided to try an experiment. So one day, this vast brilliance shot millions and millions of tiny pieces of Itself, like dazzling shooting stars, in all directions throughout the universe, creating a light show like none other. And each of these aspects of the One went on an incredible journey through solar systems and beyond, traveling farther and farther from the Source, and then returning to be reunited in a magnificent celebration of Light. From this experiment, ALL THAT IS was able to experience Itself as individuated units of consciousness and could therefore view the Whole from other perspectives and hence come to know Itself more fully.

When they began their journey, each spark of Light had full remembrance that it was a part of ALL THAT IS. However, as they journeyed farther and farther from the Source they took on more form, more density, and they began to forget that they were a part of the One. On and on they spun through time and space, ever condensing, ever materializing, until finally they reached the point of maximum separation. Everything that had taken them to that point was part of what they had become as unique crystallizations of energy. If this entire journey from the Source and back took one day on the Cosmic clock, this moment would be high noon. And from this point on each individualized aspect of ALL THAT IS begins its journey home, with ever-increasing recognition and knowingness of the Light.

The planet Earth is one such unit of consciousness. For eons it has been condensing into matter. But twelve noon has just past. More good news: We are going home!

There have been many veils in place and energies present to maintain the illusion of separation, the illusion that we are not all part of the One Magnificent Light. It is time for those veils to be lifted as more light is shed on this plane.

There was much support for the planet in reaching its point of maximum separation, and so too is there much support in bringing her home. That is why we are here. This is an exciting time, and many universal beings from other planets and other dimensions are focusing their energies on the Earth plane at this time.

—— Planet Earth ——
Distortional Limitation System 101

As the planet was condensing, beings had the option of coming here to experience a limitation system – a system based on the denial of their own Magnificence. Then, as the veils were lifted, they would experience more knowingness, more love and recognition of ALL THAT IS than ever before and their journey home could be filled with ecstasy and joy.

As you can imagine, a tremendous amount is required of the beings who chose this path. To enter into such a system, you need to forget that you are one with the Source, and that *you* decided to come here. You need to leave behind an existence based on Love and come to a place that allows fear, pain and suffering, judgment and denial, separation, abandonment, death and destruction. Nothing could have prepared you for this, and for many it was devastating. At the core of your beingness, you felt abandoned by ALL THAT IS as you experienced the pain of separation. And from that place you built a reality based on fear for your very survival. BUT YOU WERE NOT ALONE. We have always been with you, watching over you, waiting for THIS MOMENT to come.

And now, as the Earth is moving into its homeward voyage, there is the opportunity to shed these limitations and to master expression of your own Divine Spirit. As each being releases these condensed energies during this time of transition, more light will be available upon this planet, resulting in a greater expression of Love and Brilliance than ever before.

—— Planetary Transitioning ——

On a planetary scale, a massive shift is taking place. Huge infusions of light are coming to the Earth plane as the veils of separation and denial are lifting. Many of you chose to come here at this time to assist in the transition.

First, you had to go unconscious and forget who you were, or why you were here. Then you had to engage with a totally distortional system and identify yourself as a struggling human. It was then your job to wake up and begin the process of transmuting all of these distortions and patterns that are no longer functional or desired in the co-creation of a new a world.

And remember – you volunteered for the job. If you hadn't had complete faith in your own strength and courage, you wouldn't be here now. You are not alone. You have more support than you could ever possibly imagine. We send you much love at this time.

The Wake-Up Call

And as the earth passes twelve noon on the Cosmic Clock and is no longer condensing into matter but is returning home to the Source, so too are all life forms on this planet in various stages of radical transformation. The planet is mutating, and so are the beings on it. There is a *transmutation* taking place in the very cells of your body. Information that was coded into the DNA of your structure is now being activated. That is why so many of you are now waking up and remembering. It was predetermined that you would do so at this time! Beings who have been living in dense physical bodies now have the option of living in wondrous bodies of Light.

Transmutation
Dense Physical Bodies Into Light

These are very exciting times and many incredible changes are now taking place. Most of you will have been experiencing them on one level or another. We would like to discuss some of these changes so you may have more understanding of the depth of what is happening. Remember, your own experiences will be determined by your particular function and design, so they may not look anything like what we describe here. We do not wish to alarm you with all this talk of transmutation, but instead would like to gently prepare you for what is now occurring –

because these changes *are* taking place. Even scientists are beginning to admit that "something" is going on. They are discovering new proteins in the body, for example, that they think they must have overlooked before. However, they *are* new proteins.... And that is just the beginning.

The Quickening

You are high–energy transformers, like sponges in the energy sea around you. As more and more light becomes available to you, the intensity of electromagnetic energy around you also increases. Any changes in the surrounding energetic field are picked up by the subtle or etheric body, which acts as a receiver, assimilator and transmitter of these energies. These changes directly affect the physical body, which is the outward manifestation of the etheric level.

What is happening to many of you right now is that due to the increased energies present, the etheric body is vibrating at a higher frequency, and the physical body is trying to catch up but hasn't quite done so yet. This results in a speeding up of your molecular structure. Many are now experiencing this as a quickening taking place within your own bodies. This stepping up of energies is affecting every system – nerves, muscles, vessels, skin, organs and glands as they try to adapt to these new frequencies. The nervous system, which carries those energies throughout the body in the form of nerve impulses, and the endocrine system, which regulates much of your physiological functioning through the secretion of various chemical substances (hormones), may be experiencing tremendous energy overloads as they constantly attempt to maintain a state of homeostasis and balance in the body.

The Chakras As Transmitters and Receivers

As we have mentioned, the etheric body acts as a transmitter and receiver for the surrounding energies. This takes place via specific centers or *chakras.* Each chakra is directly associated with an endocrine gland and a nerve plexus. Because of their close relationship with the chakras, which transmit and receive this energy, the endocrine and nervous systems especially, are now undergoing radical transmutation. The increase in electrical energies is requiring a complete re-wiring of the nervous system, while all the organs and glands in the body are being totally restructured. In fact, as you take on a body of light, most of these organs and glands will no longer be needed, and will gradually atrophy and disappear. However, in the meantime it is important to acknowledge the changes taking place, and to support the physical body as much as possible.

Restructuring the Endocrine System

Certain energy centers will be affected more than others at different times as the shifts take place. For example, the base, or first chakra is in many of you being radically transformed at this present time. It manifests externally in the physical body as the adrenal glands, which are related to security and survival and determine your ability to deal with stress.

As they are transmuting, there may be periods when you feel more anxious and irritable than usual; feel restless, headachy, less able to concentrate; have an increased sensitivity to people, sounds, smells and environments; and experience muscle soreness (particularly low back), joint pains or poor digestion. When these glands are excessively stimulated, the body is constantly in a hyper state of "fight or flight" and expends resources at tremendous rates of speed. Therefore, during these times the body may require certain nutrients – fats, proteins, carbohydrates, vitamins, minerals and hormones – that it didn't need before. So you may experience intense cravings for certain foods, some of which you may not normally eat!

In addition, you may occasionally experience disruption to the digestive system, resulting in stomach ache, gas or bloating partly due to the increased intensity of energy in the third, or solar plexus chakra.

The fifth, or throat chakra is also a very powerful center, and its physical counterpart, the thyroid gland, is particularly vulnerable to changes in electromagnetic energy. This gland regulates the metabolic processes of the body, and in many cases is trying its hardest to keep up with the increasing vibratory rates. Some of the transmutative symptoms that commonly result are unexplained weight gain or loss, sluggishness, altered sleep patterns, and, again, feeling more tired and fatigued than usual for no apparent reason.

These are just examples of some of the things you may be experiencing as a new blueprint is being laid down for the physical body. ***The very structure of every cell in your body is changing.*** This could also be cause for periods of exhaustion as your body goes through radical remodeling and rebuilding. When this happens...just relax. Honor the changes that are taking place. Read a good book or watch a movie. And know that this, too, will pass.

—— New Pathways ——
Rewiring the Nervous System

The body picks up the energies moving in, around and through it via sensory nerves which carry impulses from the peripheral systems of the body into the grey matter of the Central Nervous System.

All is well as long as the stimuli going into the Central Nervous System are weak, as measured by the rate at which the nerve receptors fire. Strong stimuli have the effect of inhibiting normal physiological process.

As more and more light becomes available, the intensity of electromagnetic energy around you also increases. This means that there will be more rapid neurological activity in the body resulting in higher intensity impulses firing into the Central Nervous System, which will immediately attempt to dissipate that energy by sending it back out of the spinal chord.

If these impulses then fire along facilitated pathways into the muscular system, they could cause muscle tightness and soreness. If they fire into the blood vessels, restricted circulation often results. When these impulses fire into the skin, you may experience abnormal thermal sensations (feeling unusually hot or cold), prickling, itching etc. And if they should fire into the organs and glands, they may inhibit their previously normal functioning in some of the ways we have already discussed.

We can therefore see the importance of supporting the nervous system at this time as it tries to maintain a state of homeostasis in the physical body, yet at the same time "catch up" with the increased frequencies of the subtle body.

One way to do this is to interrupt some of these pathways that the high intensity impulses are travelling along, because just as someone who touches a live electric wire is held there by the current until it is switched off, so too will the structures and tissues of the body remain in a stimulated state until these pathways are interrupted, hence turning off the current. There are many transition team members now among you working with advanced technologies that utilize sound, touch, breath and movement (and other modalites), to do just that, while assisting in the creation of new pathways that are better able to utilize the higher vibrational frequencies, allowing more Light to be integrated into the physical body.

Seeing Beyond the Veils

These increased energies will not only affect the physical body. All aspects of your being are involved in the transmutation that is taking place. With the higher vibrational frequencies will come increased awareness on all levels. Many of you are still relying on old perceptual references for what is so. However, as your multidimensional awareness increases and as the veils are lifted, you will have more experiences of seeing beyond them. You may have moments of "slipping out of time and space." Some of you have experienced this already when at times it may seem like hours have gone by, but you discover that only a few minutes of linear time have passed. And the opposite happens when time just disappears and you don't know where it went. You may feel like you have been caught in a time warp.

Time can speed up and go by faster and faster and then ... the world stops in an eternal moment that lasts forever.

Embrace Your Wholeness

As each spark of Light left the Source and condensed deeper and deeper into matter and limitation, it made certain choices, certain decisions based on what was happening around it. And as they all did so, the configuration of energies that made up each individualized unit of consciousness was totally unique. Like a snowflake that falls from the sky, none was like any other, and each had its own perfect Divine Design.

You are one of those sparks of consciousness. And while experiencing limitation, many of you interpreted your uniquenesses as things that were wrong with you and set about trying to "fix" them. However, as you discovered, they are part of your core structure. You can try to manipulate and control these aspects of self, but they never really change. That's because they are not something that is wrong with you, but part of your design. The only thing that needs to change is your positioning toward them. By seeing them as what's right, what is absolutely wonderfully perfect about you, they may become your greatest assets and strengths in the new world.

By honoring your Divine Design, you are honoring your Wholeness. By honoring your Wholeness, it is easier to recognize the Oneness of all life.

Transmuting Pathways in Consciousness

Each of you, in your uniqueness, will be more attuned to certain energies than others. Like having an antenna calibrated to receive a particular station, many of you will resonate with different wavelengths, different vibrational frequencies than others. Whatever wavelengths your particular design is calibrated to are pathways cut in consciousness. Once you have begun to transmute the energies of those particular frequencies, the universe will take advantage of these pathways to transmute more and more of the same energies. So it may *appear* that issues you thought you had dealt with and resolved have suddenly re-emerged bigger than life, with even more intensity and drama than ever before. It is useful not to identify it as being your stuff. Recognize that energies are present and let them move through you. Know that you are transmuting them for the many who are not yet conscious enough to do it for themselves. That is what being a planetary transition team member is all about.

As this takes place, there may be moments when waves of grief or sadness move through you. Things you once valued that are no longer supportive are leaving your energy field. Whole aspects of a life that no longer works for you are falling away.

Remember that consciousness is energy, emotions are energy, thoughts and feelings are energy. As you integrate higher frequencies, all aspects of self will undergo major shifts and changes. Honor the magnitude of what is taking place. Honor and embrace your physical, emotional and mental bodies. For the most part they do not know what is going on, or what to do with the increased energies. From *their* perspective it may appear as if things are falling apart on all levels. Be compassionate with yourself. Remember that within this lifetime there is more evolution taking place in your body than in the total of all previous lifetimes on this planet! A *transmutation* is taking place. The very cell structure of your body is changing to enable you to withstand and integrate these higher frequencies. Your body needs to know it is okay. It has never experienced being in a Light Body before on this dimension.

—— Pattern Breaking ——

Your mental, physical and emotional bodies are wonderful barometers for Spirit, and each are vehicles through which All That Is expresses on this plane. However, in a limitation system where energies were condensing and many veils were in place, much of this valuable data from Spirit was denied, especially from the emotional body.

When an emotional experience is repressed, its vibratory rate becomes slower and slower until it goes below a conscious level and forms a dark energetic crystal, with the *entire experience* compressed and stored in the nervous system, soft tissues, organs and glands of the body. There it lies dormant, waiting to be reactivated at a later time.

There are a number of ways in which these dark crystals can then be triggered – the tonality in someone's voice, the way a person looks or acts, a smell, a thought, a touch, a feeling. Once triggered, the vibratory rate of the crystallized energy speeds up and is brought back to consciousness. At that point, although things will appear very real to you, you are actually caught up in a re-run, and are *reacting* to karmically repressed energies that have been contained in the cells of your body.

And now, as the quickening takes place and your body begins to vibrate at more refined frequencies, these repressed, denied aspects also quicken and become amplified. They need to vibrate out.

There are many advanced technologies which will shatter these energetic crystals held in the body, therefore breaking the chain of events that would lead to them manifesting around you. The use of sound is one such tool that acts as a third–dimensional access point for energies from the other dimensions to enter into this one. Touch, color, light, breath and movement can also be used as doorways through which these energies can be accessed to release dark energetic crystals into the light and to restructure patterns of consciousness that will then support your highest expression.

As more of you awaken to your Divine Mission and Purpose here, we suspect that many new and powerful technologies will be brought forth.

Remember, if all the dense, crystallized energies held in your body were released into the Light, you would have – a Light Body!

So be authentic with your emotions. As well as being barometers for, and feedback from, Spirit, they are also *energy in motion*. When you stop that motion, you create more density in your body. To live in a state of grace means that you must let go of the denial and honor all aspects of your beingness. It means that you must fully embrace your Wholeness – your feelings as well as your thoughts, intuition and knowingness – and let go of everything that says "no" to that.

Honor your emotional, physical and mental bodies so they may all work together in harmony, in support of your vision. Allow them full creative expression within their own Divine uniqueness.

—— More —— Transmutative Symptoms

As the shifts take place and your body begins to vibrate at another frequency, there may be times when it feels denser and heavier than usual, although no noticeable physical changes have taken place. Or you may feel suddenly much lighter as energies are released and shed. At times it may even feel like you have stepped into someone else's body!

Mood swings are also symptomatic of the body's attempts to integrate more light. There may be moments when you feel wonderful and have a great deal of energy, followed by a sudden crash and depression as you experience the pull of the old world.

Other reactions to the increased intensity are flu-like symptoms, sinusitis and congestion, non-specific aches and pains, and feelings of toxicity. When this happens, the body is reaching a threshold. Soon it will pass beyond this as its capacity to handle more light increases. At these times especially it is useful to drink lots of water. There is a sloughing off taking place on a cellular level. Water helps to facilitate this – both drinking and bathing. So take more baths. Go swimming. Water is wonderful to balance your energy, to soothe and relax.

Headaches and sudden shooting pains in the head or eyes are often signs that adjustments are being made, attuning you to different frequencies. Parts of the brain that have been dormant are now being called to use. Often that requires some rewiring of the circuitry. At the same time, brain patterns that are no longer functional are rerouted. Many transition team members have access to technologies that will greatly facilitate these shifts.

Ringing or tones in the ears are often transmissions from other dimensions. This information often makes itself known to you at the appropriate time.

Sometimes you might be in the middle of a sentence when suddenly ... you completely forget what you were going to say next. Or you may be thinking about something that happened when ... you have difficulty accessing the memory of it. The more we move into a state of grace, the harder it is to reference the past. In fact all useless data is gradually being taken from the files. In mastering limitation, past referencing was useful, because what you accepted as reality was based on your beliefs and experiences. Now things can be so because you *know* them to be so. Referencing to the past is falling away. We no longer have to keep it alive. NOW is the time.

Also, you may be fully engaged in something, totally enthused by it, when...the energy is gone, your interest has died. This could be a message from Spirit that there is no longer alignment with what you are doing, and it is not the highest possibility for where your energies and attention could be. So Spirit simply pulls the plug. Therefore, it is useful to pay close attention to the energies present in every moment, and to do only that which makes your heart sing!

— A New Context for Healing —

We mention these symptoms because many of you are experiencing them as something that is wrong with you that needs to be "fixed," and go running off looking for someone or something to heal you. We don't think you need to be healed because we don't think there is anything *wrong* with you. All is in alignment with the Divine Plan. If you identify with what you think is wrong with you, you may find yourself going down with the part that is dying. Therefore, we suggest that you do not become overly fascinated with these symptoms, but instead recognize them as part of an evolutionary process that is taking place.

However, discernment is required. If you do think you need medical assistance, there are many in the healing professions (bodyworkers, acupuncturists, homeopaths and naturopaths, for example) who are conscious of these shifts and may be of support to you.

— Discernment —

Speaking of discernment, we would like to point out that many of these symptoms of evolution could also be symptoms of you not following your own Spirit. Or they may indicate that undermining energies are present.

As the planet was condensing, traveling further and further from the Source, certain energies and entities came here to assist the planet in reaching its point of maximum separation so it could then return Home. However, just like some transition team members, many of the beings holding these energies in place have forgotten who they are, and why they are here. Now is the time for those entities and energies to be released to the Light. It is time for them to go Home, too. If you suspect the presence of disembodied spirits with you, there are powerful depossession techniques now available to escort them into the Light.

Have faith in your own knowing, and never underestimate it. Doubt is symptom number one of undermining energies, and is not a natural state to be in. Follow whatever you think is your Spirit until you know otherwise. Even if it later turns out you are wrong – so what? It is better to be wrong than to doubt your own truth.

—— Supporting Your Body —— During the Shifts

As you can see, your body's needs will probably change rapidly during these times. We have already mentioned that you may have weird cravings for foods you don't normally eat. Also, you may have a huge appetite one day and hardly be hungry the next. You might find yourself sleeping many more hours than usual and having to take naps during the day, and then needing very little sleep at all and having an abundance of energy. What's most important is to stay in touch moment to moment. You body will guide you to the foods and support it needs. All you have to do is listen to it.

We already mentioned the importance of drinking lots of water. Physical exercise is also extremely supportive, be it walking, jogging, running, hiking, swimming, or dancing. The latter is particularly powerful because through movement and dance many new energetic pathways can be cut and integrated throughout the body.

Make use of conscious bodyworkers that can assist in releasing energies that are held in a crystalline matrix within the structures and tissues of the body. Connective tissue work is especially useful for this; also, neuromuscular therapy, which helps repattern and "open" the nervous system as well as break down crystallized energy. Cranial-sacral therapy can also be supportive in integrating these new energies. When done in conjunction with sound, bodywork is especially effective.

As the increased energies are being integrated into the body, some of you may benefit from chiropractic adjustments, as there may be periods when you are more prone to distortions and subluxations of the spine due to the changes taking place. There are also many homeopathic, gem and Bach remedies that you may find supportive to the emotional and physical bodies.

— Divine Timing —

As the planet makes its shift and journeys back to the Source, ultimately everyone who chooses to stay here and remain in a body will also go through these shifts. However, each person has his/her own "high noon." Some beings passed noon many centuries ago; others will not reach it for many years to come. Therefore, it is important to honor the Divine Timing of these shifts and changes. You may find that some patterns are not ready to be released yet. Again, honor your Wholeness. Recognize that it is all part of the Divine Plan unfolding.

— The Starseeds — For a New Civilization

As you go through this period of transitioning from the old world that is dying to the new that is emerging, there may be times when you feel "out of phase" or "disjointed" as you let go of the old, when the new has not yet fully formed. This can be especially frustrating for the mental and emotional bodies. You may feel less and less functional as the *old world* has defined it. This has a tendency to lower your self-esteem and bring up all sorts of survival issues. Recognize that survival is NOT the issue. You didn't come here to merely survive. You have a job to do, and part of that job is transmuting distortional patterns that you have taken on. And as you do so, you are cutting pathways and transmuting them for many. It's not personal; it's not your stuff. See it from a vaster perspective. ***You are the forerunners, the starseeds for a new civilization.***

And as you transition more and more into following your Spirit without hesitation, doing everything in each and every moment because you were Divinely guided to do so as opposed to following your ego/personality's wishes, you will find your life to be *more* ecstatic, *more* joyous, *more* emotional, *more* passionate, *more* intense, *more* dramatic than ever before. Transpersonal does *not* mean boring!

The Birth of a New Era

So here you are in the midst of great changes – in fact, *the* most radical period of change in this planet's history. The old world is dying. It must and will happen, so let it do so gracefully. As more and more of the energies from other dimensions enter into this plane, much of what you have known and held on to will gradually fall away, giving birth to a new, higher octave of expression.

Many will cling to and try to "save" the old world that is dying, for though it is filled with illusions of duality and separation, it is familiar, and to step into the new world often means leaping into the Unknown.

One of the most important keys in making this transition is to pay attention to what your fascinations are – *to everything you consciously, and unconsciously, accept as reality.* What do you make real in your life? What do you focus your energies on?

Consider for a moment that what you have previously thought of as real is nothing more than an audiovisual hologram of consciousness – in other words, a *picture* of reality. You think in pictures, and it is from these pictures that your inner reality is formed. Everything you do, how you think, feel and act, and what you manifest in the world around you, is affected by the pictures you hold as true.

Throughout your life you have been bombarded with other people's pictures of reality – parents, teachers, friends and peers – as well as those coded in the cell structures of your body genetically and from past lives.

All those images that you agreed with as being *the way that life is* have become stored in the conscious and unconscious mind and form the basis for your current reality. Many of you don't see them as *optional* images, or pictures of reality, but consider them "real." However, these pictures *are* optional. You *can* change them.

In fact, to fully engage in the new world requires that you be conscious moment to moment of what you consider real and of what you put your attention on. All That Is, in Its desire to love and support you wants you to have it all, and presumes that your attention is on what you want. It will therefore rearrange Itself to manifest even more of the same. Whatever you lend your fascination to, whatever you label or define as reality, you'll get more of.

If you focus your energies on that which is dying, you will only prolong the inevitable.

For a time you may feel the pull of the old world reality, but if you recognize the illusions and *do not accept them as your reality*, remembering instead the magnificence of your *true identity*, you will experience more and more ease in being completely and wholly engaged with the new species and civilization that is emerging – a civilization based on love, not fear. A civilization of beings who live an ecstatic existence in bodies of Light, exploring the mastery of Divine Expression. Proclaim *this* as your vision. Live it as your reality. Focus your attention on it. Set it alight with the fire of purpose. Make a big deal out of all the things in your life that are in alignment with your vision. Destroy all the pictures and illusions that do not support its fullest expression. Take a stand for it in all areas of your life. Then All That Is will rearrange itself to bring you even more of your version of Heaven on Earth.

The Gathering of Masters

The time we have been waiting for is now upon us. There is a Great Gathering taking place. Planet Earth has become a focal point throughout this universe and beyond. Due to the incredible diversity of species here, many beings from other planets and dimensions are offering their support and assistance at this time. Many Councils, Federations, Alliances and Commands are now coming together as the Divine Plan unfolds.

A great number of beings presently incarnated on this plane are aspects of and representatives or focal points for whole councils of entities on the other dimensions. ***It is time to wake up to the vast multidimensional master that you are.*** Yes, you are human, but you are also *so much more*. You came here with a Divine Mission. Part of that was to go unconscious and forget who you were and why you were here. Now is the time to remember. Stand up and step forward into the Light of your Magnificence. Embody all that you truly are. The time that you have been preparing for is NOW. In your uniqueness you have access to skills and technologies, many of which have never been available on this planet before. You each have a contribution to make in the co-creation of this New World. And no matter how insignificant you may think your piece is, you all hold a key. Remember, it may be the smallest piece of the jigsaw puzzle, but if it is the last piece, it becomes the most important, and the picture isn't complete until ALL the pieces are in place.

—— Your Seed Vision —— Leads You Home

All that is required of you is that you take that initial leap, that leap into the Unknown. Sooner or later you will all face that choice. And if you are lucky, there will be no choice. For a voice is calling you. It is Your Voice. It tells you to look within. And there, in each of you, is a Seed Vision which speaks of something you have longed for, ached for, burned for. Something that has always carried you forth when it appeared as if all the odds were stacked against you. Something that has called out to that precious part deep within you, giving you faith, courage and strength to go on. That piece ... is the Spark of Light ... which will lead you Home. And there we joyously wait for you, arms outstretched, with tears of Love in our eyes. And then you will *know* that we have always been with you ... every step of the way.

We love you ... and we welcome you Home.

Golden Star Alliance.

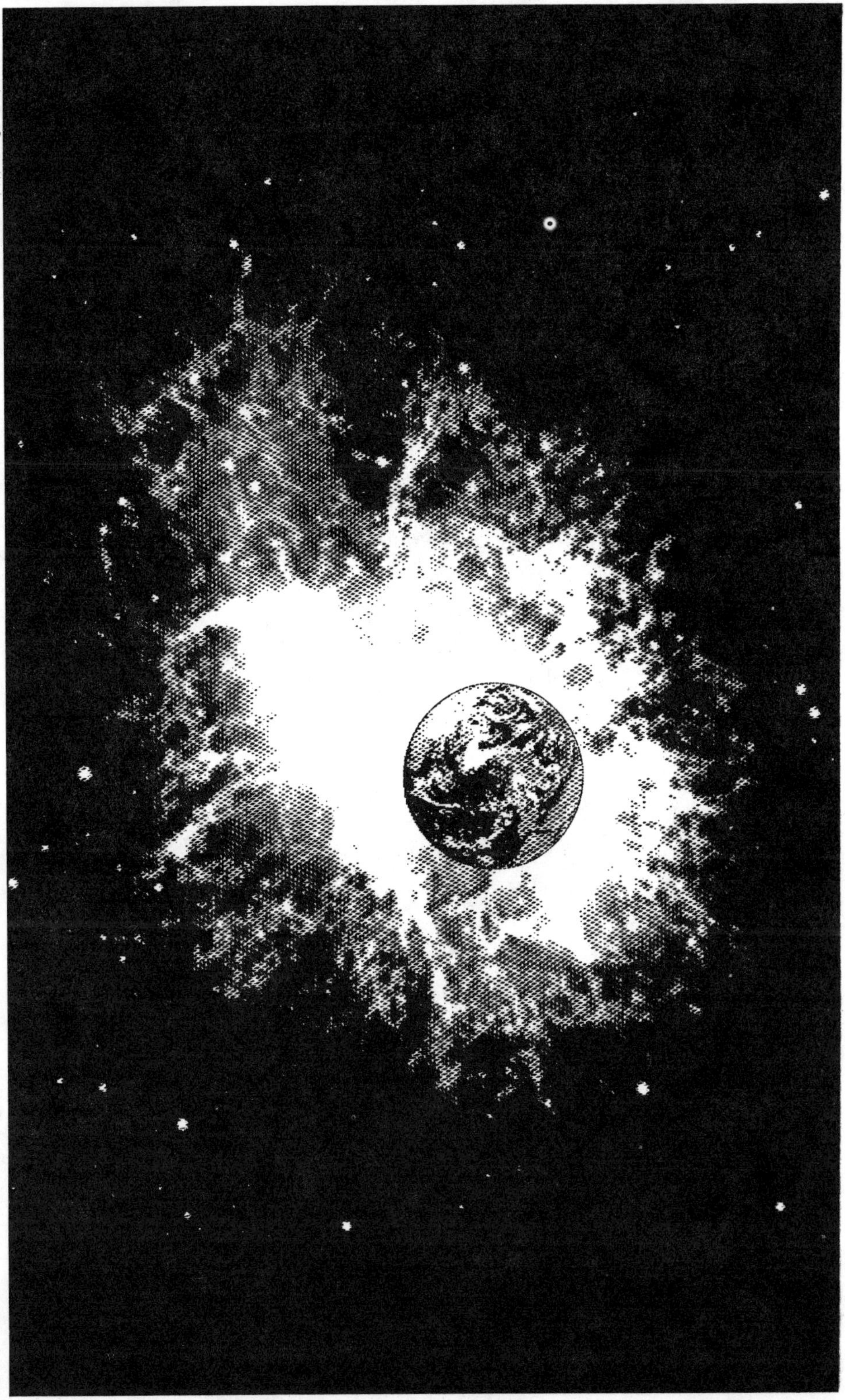

THE GOLDEN STAR ALLIANCE ...

...is an aspect of the Council of the Stellar Ring. This is a vast intergalactic council whose members are both extraterrestrial and angelic in origin, and also includes an Ascended Master who originally sourced from planet Earth. Most of the beings on this council had dense, third dimensional bodies at one time, which, through the process of Ascension, they transformed into immortal bodies of Light. Now, those beings have gathered together to support the evolution of planets. They are specialists in supporting beings in living lives dedicated to Spirit.

The Council of the Stellar Ring are focusing their energies and attention on Planet Earth at this time, to assist in it's ecstatic transformation into a Star.

The words on these pages hold no eternal significance. They are but a focalization, an access point, for the energies we are transmitting to enter your realm. We will remain with you, and make ourselves available for any adjustments your Spirit has requested be made at this time.

We are with you every step of the way.

In Light and Love,

Council of the Stellar Ring

The following is a list of services currently offered by ZāRah and the Golden Star Alliance:

—— One and Two Day Events ——
"Living as a Master"

The focus of these events will be to support the ecstatic transformation that is taking place. Together we will *ACTIVATE pre-encoded cellular memories that your spirit has requested be activated at this time, while assisting you in the *INTEGRATION of these higher vibrational frequencies so you may incorporate more Light into your body with ease and grace. We will also *RELEASE patterns and energies that are no longer functional in supporting your highest expression.

These events may include any of the following...

- ✦ Pattern Breaking
- ✦ Depossession Techniques
- ✦ Light Code Activation
- ✦ Data Transmission
- ✦ Channeled Fifth Dimensional Energies, Insights and Awareness
- ✦ And many other Advanced Technologies of Consciousness...

...to assist you in incorporating more of the Master that you are on the other dimensions into your day-to-day existence on this one. They are designed to powerfully catapult you into your next octave of expression in living as a Master here on Planet Earth.

They will support you in...

- ✦ Living as a Master
- ✦ Loving Your Wholeness
- ✦ Coming closer to your own Spirit
- ✦ Fulfilling your Divine Mission and Purpose here
- ✦ Taking a stand for your vision of Heaven on Earth

- ✦ Leaving behind a reality that no longer works for or supports you
- ✦ Following your Spirit without hesitation in the co-creation of a New World with other Masters
- ✦ Stepping forth into the Magnificence of Who You Truly Are

THESE POWERFUL EVENTS
WILL RADICALLY SHIFT YOUR REALITY !
Each is totally unique and Divinely guided by Spirit.

If you are interested in becoming a local coordinator and hosting an event in your area, please contact Golden Star Alliance at the address below.

—— Private Sessions ——

These may include any of the event services listed, in addition to ...

- ✦ Hands-on Data Transfer
- ✦ Energetic Re-wiring
- ✦ Integration of Higher Vibrational Frequencies

—— Mailing List Update ——

If you wish to be on our mailing list and receive information about further publications, newsletters and audio tapes, or would like to be notified of upcoming events in your area, please send your name, address and phone number to the following address.

Our new address:
Golden Star Alliance
1410 Forest Dr. #8, Suite 133
Annapolis, MD 21403
(800) 576-1669

Many of the models and technologies of consciousness discussed in this book were originally presented by Extraterrestrial Earth Mission.

Further information about these technologies is available in the E. T. Master's Tool Kit. From our perspective, this is one of the most valuable tools available on the planet to assist beings in making the transition from one reality they have been living, to another that more fully expresses who they are. It consists of:

Shattering Illusions - Setting yourself free from dysfunctional pictures of reality

The Superconscious Technique - Allows for an experience of aligning with your Spirit in your day-to-day life

Conscious Channeling
An Extraterrestrial Approach

Transcending the 4th Dimension
A "light" approach to exorcism

YOU ARE NOT ALONE...
...WE HAVE ALWAYS BEEN WITH YOU,
WATCHING OVER YOU,
WAITING FOR THIS MOMENT TO COME.

ZāRah and the Golden Star Alliance
gratefully acknowledge

ZaviRah'and Ziva'rah
Alarius and friends

Zarina
and
the Golden Light Synergy

and
Neilaza

For all their love and support